T0402756

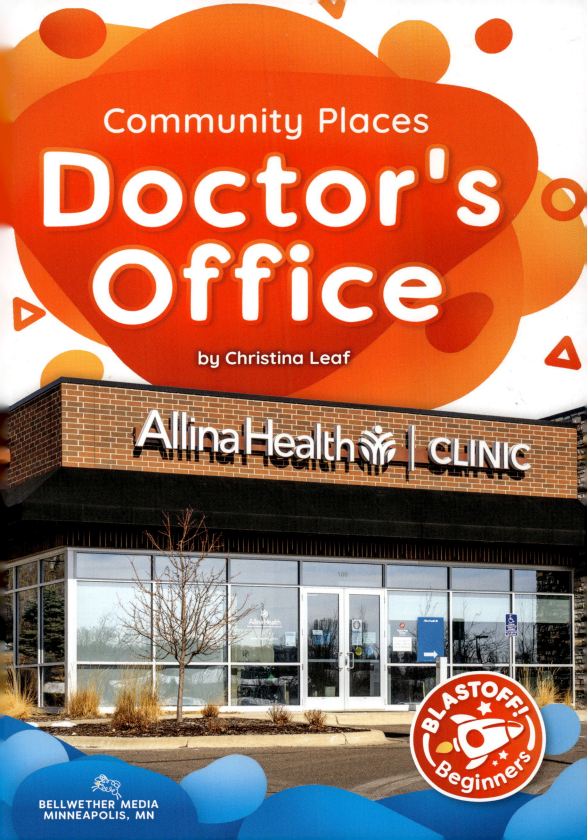

Community Places

Doctor's Office

by Christina Leaf

Allina Health | CLINIC

BELLWETHER MEDIA
MINNEAPOLIS, MN

BLASTOFF!
Beginners

Blastoff! Beginners are developed by literacy experts and educators to meet the needs of early readers. These engaging informational texts support young children as they begin reading about their world. Through simple language and high frequency words paired with crisp, colorful photos, Blastoff! Beginners launch young readers into the universe of independent reading.

Blastoff! Universe

Reading Level — Grade K

Grades 1-3

Grade 4

Sight Words in This Book 🔍

a	for	is	see	time
an	from	it	sit	to
are	here	look	the	we
at	how	may	these	well
do	if	out	they	
find	in	people	this	

This edition first published in 2023 by Bellwether Media, Inc.

No part of this publication may be reproduced in whole or in part without written permission of the publisher. For information regarding permission, write to Bellwether Media, Inc., Attention: Permissions Department, 6012 Blue Circle Drive, Minnetonka, MN 55343.

Library of Congress Cataloging-in-Publication Data

LC record for Doctor's Office available at: https://lccn.loc.gov/2022036345

Text copyright © 2023 by Bellwether Media, Inc. BLASTOFF! BEGINNERS and associated logos are trademarks and/or registered trademarks of Bellwether Media, Inc.

Editor: Rebecca Sabelko   Designer: Gabriel Hilger

Printed in the United States of America, North Mankato, MN.

Table of Contents

At the Doctor's Office!

It is time for a **checkup**. We are at the doctor's office!

4

What Are Doctors' Offices?

Doctors' offices are important places. They keep us healthy!

A Visit to the Doctor

Patients sit in the waiting room.

waiting room

patients

Nurses check
how tall people are.
They weigh people.

nurse

Nurses may give shots. These keep us from being sick!

13

This is an **exam room**. Doctors see patients here.

exam room

doctor

Doctors do tests.
They look at eyes.
They look in ears.

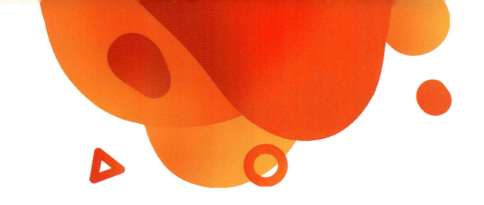

Doctors find out
if people are sick.
They **treat** people.

18

Going to the doctor's office keeps us well!

Doctor's Office Facts

At the Doctor's Office

doctor

patient

exam room

What Happens at a Doctor's Office?

nurses give shots

doctors do tests

doctors treat people

Glossary

checkup

a visit to see how well people are doing

exam room

the place where doctors meet with patients

patients

people who come to see a doctor

treat

to give care to someone

To Learn More

ON THE WEB

FACTSURFER

Factsurfer.com gives you a safe, fun way to find more information.

1. Go to www.factsurfer.com.

2. Enter "doctor's office" into the search box and click 🔍.

3. Select your book cover to see a list of related content.

Index

The images in this book are reproduced through the courtesy of: Ken Wolter, front cover; StockImageFactory.com, p. 3; LaylaBird, pp. 4-5; sripfoto, p. 6; New Africa, pp. 6-7; xavierarnau, pp. 8-9; Hispanolistic, pp. 10-11; didesign021, pp. 12-13; FatCamera, pp. 14-15, 22 (at the doctor); Pollyanna Ventura, p. 16; KatarzynaBialasiewicz, pp. 16-17; undefined undefined, pp. 18-19; Pressmaster, pp. 20-21; Thurtell, p. 22 (nurses give shots); SofikoS, p. 22 (doctors do tests); Drazen Zigic, p. 22 (doctors treat people); Monkey Business Images, p. 23 (checkup); Jim Still-Pepper, p. 23 (exam room); Iryna Rahalskaya, p. 23 (patients); SDI Productions, p. 23 (treat).